# WINNING IS NOT FINAL

## A Story of Sportsmanship and Growth

## By: Emmanuel Amaugo

Written by: Emmanuel Amaugo
Illustrations and Cover Design: Emmanuel Amaugo
Edited by: Amarachi Amaugo
Publisher: Reed to Rock Ltd
ISBN: 978-1-0823-5298-0
Printed in the United Kingdom
First Edition

## Dedication

I dedicate this book to God, who gives me strength and purpose,
 and to my amazing parents, whose love, guidance, and support have shaped my journey.
 This is just the beginning of my Decade of Destiny!

# CHAPTER ONE
# The Big Discovery

The sun shone brightly over Ubakala Town, making the dusty roads shimmer like gold. Ikuku, a 10-year-old boy, and his 9-year-old sister, Ada, walked side by side, looking for cool, fresh water. It was a hot day, and the small stream near their home was nearly dry.

Suddenly, Ada stopped in her tracks.

"Ikuku, look!", she said, pointing at something ahead.

Between two tall trees, a big, colorful banner fluttered in the wind. Ikuku squinted and read the words out loud:

"NEXT WEEK: THE Ubakala GRAND RACE! Open to All! A Special Prize for the Winner!"

Ada's eyes lit up. "A race? A real competition?"

Ikuku's heart pounded with excitement. "Yes! And we can enter!"

Ada grinned. "I've been racing for four years, and you're one of thefastest kids in school.
We have to do this!"
Without wasting a second, they sprinted home to tell their parents.

At home, their mother, Mrs Eze, was cooking, and their father, Mr Eze, was fixing a wooden chair.

"Mama! Papa!" Ada shouted, nearly out of breath.

"What is it?" Mrs Eze asked.

Ikuku held up his hands excitedly. "There's going to be a big race in town next week! Can we enter?"

Mr Eze stroked his chin. "A race, you say? Are you both sure you want to do this?"

"Yes!", Ikuku and Ada said at the same time.

Their parents smiled.

"Alright", Mrs Eze said. "We will sign you up!" "YES!", the children cheered.

That night, Ikuku lay in bed, staring at the ceiling.

"I will win", he whispered to himself.

On the other side of the room, Ada smiled in the dark.

"I will run my best", she thought.

Neither of them knew it yet, but this race would change everything.

# CHAPTER TWO
# Training Begins

The next morning, Ubakala School was buzzing with excitement. Everyone had heard about the Grand Race.

At the assembly, Mrs Chidi, the headmistress, stepped forward. "Children, I know many of you want to enter the race", she said. "But only a few students from our school can make it to the qualifying rounds". A wave of whispers filled the air. Students shifted nervously, eager to see who would be chosen.

Ikuku and Ada exchanged worried glances.

One by one, students wrote their names and dropped them into the large glass jar. The atmosphere was electric with anticipation.

Mrs Chidi stirred the papers and reached inside.

"The first name is... Chika!" The crowd cheered as Chika stepped forward, beaming.

"And the second name is… Michael!" More applause as Michael waved.

Ikuku's heart raced. The suspense was building as Mrs Chidi continued to pull names.

"Next we have… Ada!" Ada gasped, her face lighting up. "I made it!"

The crowd cheered, but Ikuku still wasn't chosen. The tension was thick as Mrs Chidi reached for the final slip.

"And the last name is… Ikuku!". "YES!",Ikuku shouted, pumping his fist in the air.

The crowd erupted with cheers as Ikuku and Ada grinned at each other. They had made it to the qualifying rounds, but they weren't the only ones, many others had a chance, too.

That evening, their parents called Coach Nkuzi, the best trainer in Ubakala.

"Training starts on Monday at Ubakala Community Square", he told them. "Be ready!"

Ikuku and Ada could hardly wait.

On Monday afternoon, they arrived at the training grounds. Other young racers stood nearby, stretching and warming up, ready to prove themselves.

Coach Nkuzi, a tall, powerful man with kind eyes, clapped his hands.

"Alright, racers! Start with five laps around the track!"

Ada paced herself, keeping a steady rhythm. But Ikuku had a different plan. He thought, "I'll beat them all", and sprinted ahead. One by one, he passed the others, leaving only Ada in the lead.

"Oh, hi Ikuku!", Ada teased.

Ikuku gritted his teeth. "I'll pass you!", he said under his breath.

He chased her instead of focusing on his own pace, turning the training into a race.

Coach Nkuzi's voice boomed, "Ikuku! Ada! This is not a game! Training is about control and discipline!".

Ikuku lowered his head.

He thought winning was everything. But was it?

# CHAPTER THREE
# Ikuku's Obsession

The days passed quickly, and training became harder. Coach Nkuzi made them do laps, sprints, and strength exercises.

"Speed alone won't win a race", he reminded them. "You need stamina, strategy, and self-control".

Ada listened carefully and followed instructions. She paced herself, saving energy for the final sprint.

But Ikuku, he had only one goal, to win.

One afternoon, Coach Nkuzi set up a practice race.

"Racers, on your marks", he shouted.

Ikuku crouched down, eyes fixed on the track.

"3... 2... 1... GO!"

Ikuku blasted forward, running as fast as his legs could carry him. He overtook one racer, then another, then another.

But by the last lap, his legs burned, and his breath came in quick gasps. Suddenly, Ada sped past him, smooth and strong.

Ikuku gritted his teeth. "No! I won't let her win!"

He pushed himself harder, but his muscles were too tired. Ada crossed the finish line first.

Ikuku slowed to a stop, panting. His chest tightened with frustration. How had Ada beaten him?

Coach Nkuzi walked over. "Ikuku, do you know why you lost?" Ikuku folded his arms. "Because I didn't run fast enough."

Coach Nkuzi shook his head. "No, you used all your energy too soon. A good racer knows when to push and when to pace."

Ikuku frowned. "But Ada won, and I want to win!"

"Winning is good", Coach Nkuzi said. "But if you only focus on being the best, you'll forget how to improve. And a staunch champion always learns".

Ikuku sighed.

He didn't like losing, especially not to Ada.

As they walked home, Ada nudged him. "Hey, don't be mad. You'll do better next time!"

Ikuku didn't answer.

Deep inside, he had already decided.

Next time, he wouldn't lose. No matter what.

# CHAPTER FOUR
## The Race Begins

After weeks of training and preliminary trials, the real competition had begun. The first stage had narrowed down the field, screening out many hopeful racers until only five remained. These five, the best from Ubakala School, had qualified for the quarter-finals of the Grand Race.

The Ubakala Community Square was filled with energy and excitement. A sea of people gathered under the afternoon sun, waving banners and cheering for their favourite racers. The quarter-finals were finally here! Ikuku and Ada stood near the starting line, stretching and warming up. Their parents, Mr Eze and Mrs Eze, watched proudly from the sidelines. "Stay focused", Mr Eze said. "And most importantly, enjoy the race!" Ada nodded with a smile. Ikuku, however, barely heard him. All he could think about was winning.

The commentator's voice boomed through the speakers.

"First race: Chinara vs. Ada!"

Ada took a deep breath and walked to the starting line. Beside her, Chinara, a tall, strong girl, looked nervous.

"Good luck", Ada said kindly.

Chinara smiled. "You too!"

The referee raised his hand.

"On your marks... Get set... GO!"

Ada sprang forward, her feet pounding against the track. She ran smoothly, keeping her breathing steady.

But Chinara was fast! She quickly closed the gap between them. The crowd roared as the racers ran side by side.

Ada's heart pounded, "I have to push harder!".

Summoning all her strength, she surged ahead, crossing the finish line just seconds before Chinara.

The stadium erupted in cheers. Ada had won!

Ikuku ran up to her. "You were amazing!"

Ada grinned. "Thanks! Now it's your turn".

Ikuku nodded confidently. "I won't lose".

The commentator called the next race:

"Obinna vs. Ikuku!"

Ikuku stepped onto the track, his heart racing, not with fear, but with determination.

As the referee raised his hand, Ikuku whispered to himself, "this is my moment".

"On your marks... Get set... GO!"

Ikuku exploded forward, his arms and legs moving as fast as lightning. Obinna tried to keep up, but Ikuku was too strong.

In just a few moments, he crossed the finish line first!

The crowd roared with excitement.

Ikuku threw his fist in the air, "I did it!", he exclaimed.

Both siblings had won their quarter-final races.

Now, the semi-finals awaited.

# CHAPTER FIVE
## The Semi-Finals

The semi-finals were here! Cheers, drums, and whistles filled the air as the crowd gathered again at Ubakala Community Square.

Ikuku and Ada stood near the track, watching as other racers competed. They both knew only two racers would make it to the Grand Finale.

"I have to win", Ikuku whispered to himself.

Ada smiled as she stretched. "No matter what happens, I'm going to do my best!"

The commentator's voice boomed through the microphone. "First semi-final: Ada vs. Kelechi!"

Ada and Kelechi, a tall, healthy boy, walked to the starting line.

Kelechi smirked, "I hope you're ready to lose, Ada".

Ada laughed playfully. "I'm just ready to run!"

The referee raised his hand.

"On your marks... Get set... GO!"

Ada took off, running smoothly and steadily.

Kelechi was fast, staying close to her. For most of the race, they were neck and neck.

Then, Ada remembered Coach Nkuzi's advice: "Save your energy for the last stretch".

Taking a deep breath, she waited for the last few seconds of the race. Then, with one last burst of speed, she sprinted forward, crossing the finish line just ahead of Kelechi!

Yes!", she cheered. She was going to the Grand Finale! Now, it was Ikuku's turn.

"Second semi-final: Ikuku vs. Emmanuel!"

Ikuku stepped up, his heart pounding. He glanced at Ada, if she had won; he had to win too.

"On your marks... Get set... GO!"

Ikuku blasted forward, putting all his strength into the race. Emmanuel was fast, but Ikuku was faster.

The crowd cheered as Ikuku pulled ahead. With one final push, he crossed the finish line first!

"YES!", he shouted.

He had done it!

Both Ikuku and Ada had made it to the Grand Finale. But now, they would have to race against each other.

# CHAPTER SIX

# The Grand Finale is Set

The semi-finals were over, and the biggest race of all was just ahead— the Grand Finale.

But there was a twist.

For the first time in the history of the Ubakala Grand Race, the final two racers were siblings.

Ikuku vs. Ada.

The crowd buzzed with excitement. People whispered and pointed at them.

"Brother against sister?" "Who will win?"

Ikuku and Ada walked off the track together, still catching their breath.

"Wow," Ada said, grinning. "We really did it!"

Ikuku nodded, but inside, he felt tense. He didn't just want to be in the final, he wanted to win.

"Good job, Ada", he said. "But tomorrow, I'm going to beat you". Ada laughed lightly. "We'll see!"

That evening, back at home, Mr Eze and Mrs Eze made a special dinner to celebrate their children's achievements.

"We are so proud of both of you," Mr Eze said, handing them fresh fruit juice.

"You have already made history", Mrs Eze added. "Tomorrow, no matter who wins, we will celebrate!"

Ada smiled. "Thanks, Mama! I just want to run my best".

But Ikuku felt unsatisfied. He stirred his food without eating.

"If I don't win, it won't mean anything", he muttered.

Mr Eze raised an eyebrow. "Winning isn't everything, Ikuku". Ikuku didn't answer.

That night, Ikuku lay in bed, staring at the ceiling.

He could hear Ada's soft breathing from the other side of the room. "She's fast... but I have to be faster".

His fists clenched.

Tomorrow, "I will win. No matter what it takes".

On the other side of the room, Ada sighed happily, thinking about how much fun she had.

Neither knew that tomorrow's race would teach them an important lesson.

# CHAPTER SEVEN

## The Grand Finale

The big day had arrived.

People packed the Ubakala Community Square. The crowd roared with excitement, waving banners and chanting the names of the two finalists.

"IKUKU! ADA! IKUKU! ADA!"

The energy in the air was electric. Even people who had never met the siblings came to watch, this was a historic race!

Ikuku and Ada stood at the starting line, side by side.

"I hope you're ready to lose, little sister", Ikuku said with a smirk. Ada just smiled. "I'm ready to run my best".

The referee raised his hand.

"Racers, on your marks!"

Ikuku took a deep breath, his muscles tensed.

"Get set…"

Ada bounced lightly on her toes, preparing for the first push forward.

"GO!"

The race began!

Ikuku exploded forward, his legs pumping fast. Ada ran smoothly, keeping pace beside him.

The crowd cheered wildly as the two sped down the track, side by side. Ikuku gritted his teeth. "I have to go faster!"

He pushed harder, using all his energy early, trying to outrun Ada.

But Ada stayed calm. She knew the race wasn't just about speed, it was about endurance, too.

The last lap approached. Ikuku was slowing down. His heavy legs and ragged breathing slowed him down.

Ada saw her chance.

With a deep breath, she surged forward, running faster than ever before.

Ikuku tried to catch up, but his legs wouldn't move any faster. With a final, powerful stride, Ada crossed the finish line first! The crowd erupted in cheers!

"THE WINNER IS ADA!", shouted the commentator.

Ikuku froze in place. His heart pounded. His hands clenched into fists.

"I... lost?" he asked under his breath.

Ada turned and smiled at him.

"Noble race, Ikuku", she said cheerfully.

But Ikuku didn't feel happy. He felt angry.

He had lost and to his little sister.

And that, he thought, was the worst feeling in the world.

# CHAPTER EIGHT

## Defeat and Disappointment

The cheers of the crowd rang through the air. People clapped, whistled, and chanted Ada's name.

"ADA! ADA! ADA!"

She stood in the centre of the track, grinning from ear to ear, as the referee held up her hand. She had won!

But Ikuku wasn't smiling.

He stood a few steps behind, his fists clenched, his chest rising and falling with heavy breaths. His heart pounded, not from the race, but from the sting of losing.

His little sister had beaten him.

It wasn't supposed to happen.

As Ada turned to him, she smiled brightly. "That was so much fun! You ran well, Ikuku!"

Ikuku's face burned. His hands curled tighter into fists.

He didn't smile back. He didn't even look at her.

Instead, he turned and walked away.

Ada's smile faded. "Ikuku?"

But he didn't answer.

Behind the finish line, Coach Nkuzi and their parents were waiting.

Mrs Eze rushed forward and hugged Ada. "We are so proud of you!"

Mr Eze patted Ikuku's shoulder. "And you too, my son. You did amazingly well."

But Ikuku shrugged him off. "No, I didn't", he muttered.

Coach Nkuzi crossed his arms. "Ikuku, what's wrong?"

Ikuku finally exploded. "I LOST! I should have won! I was supposed to be the best!"

Coach Nkuzi looked at him calmly. "Why do you think you deserved to win more than Ada?"

Ikuku opened his mouth, then shut it.

He had no answer.

33

Ada had trained just as hard as he had. She had listened to the coach, saved her energy, and ran the smarter race. And now, she was the champion.

Ikuku swallowed hard, unsure of what to say next.

Suddenly, he didn't feel angry anymore.

He just felt tired.

"Come", Coach Nkuzi said gently, "let's talk".

Ikuku sighed and nodded slowly.

Maybe losing wasn't the end.

Maybe, just maybe, he had something to learn.

# CHAPTER NINE
## A Lesson from Coach Nkuzi

Ikuku sat on the bench, staring at the ground. The excitement of the crowd faded into the background. Ada stood nearby, watching him with concern. She had expected him to be disappointed, but not this upset.

Coach Nkuzi sat down beside Ikuku. He waited a moment before speaking.

"You ran well today", the coach said.

Ikuku shook his head. "No, I didn't, I lost".

Coach Nkuzi smiled, "and what does losing mean to you?"

Ikuku frowned, "it means I wasn't good enough. It means Ada was better than me."

Coach Nkuzi nodded.

"Today, she was. But tell me, Ikuku, did you try your best?"

Ikuku hesitated, then nodded slowly. "Yes... I ran as fast as I could."

"And did you learn something?" Coach Nkuzi asked again.

Ikuku thought for a moment. He remembered how Ada had saved her energy, how she had paced herself instead of rushing.

"I... I should have been more patient", he admitted. "I used all my energy too soon".

Coach Nkuzi smiled proudly. "Exactly, that's what staunch champions do. Ikuku, they learn from every race. Winning is not final, and losing is not failure. It's just a step to becoming better".

Ikuku sat quietly, letting the words sink in.

"You're lucky, Ikuku", Coach Nkuzi continued. "You have a brilliant sister who ran her best and gave you a tough challenge. Be proud of her, just like she would be proud of you if you had won".

Ikuku looked up at Ada. She wasn't smug or bragging. She just stood there, waiting for him.

Slowly, Ikuku stood up and walked towards her.

"You ran a noble race, Ada", he said at last. "Congratulations", Ada beamed. "Thanks, Ikuku! And you were amazing too!"

For the first time since the race ended, Ikuku smiled. Maybe winning wasn't everything after all.

# CHAPTER TEN
# A New Goal

That evening, Mr Eze and Mrs Eze prepared a special celebration for both Ada and Ikuku.

A big, delicious cake sat in the middle of the table, decorated with the words:

"Congratulations, Champions!"

Ikuku looked at the cake and then at his family. They weren't just celebrating Ada, they were celebrating both of them.

Mr Eze raised his cup. "To Ada, the champion!"

"And to Ikuku," Mrs Eze added, "for running an amazing race and showing a resilient spirit!"

Ikuku smiled shyly as everyone clapped. Maybe losing wasn't so bad after all.

As they ate, Ada turned to Ikuku.

"You know", she said, "there's always next year".Ikuku looked up. "Next year?"

She nodded. "The race happens every year. And you know what?"

40

"What?",Ikuku asked.

"I think you're going to be even stronger next time", Ada said with a grin.

Ikuku thought about that. He had learned so much from this race. He had pushed himself, but now he knew how to run smarter.

Next year, he would be better prepared.

He grinned. "You know what, Ada? Next time, I'll be the one winning."

Ada laughed, "we'll see about that!"

Mr Eze and Mrs Eze chuckled. "Win or lose",Mrs Eze said, "what matters most is that you enjoy the race and try your best".

Ikuku nodded, "yeah... I get that now".

Coach Nkuzi's words echoed in his mind: "Winning is not final. Losing is not failure. Every race is just another step to becoming better."

As Ikuku lay in bed that night, he didn't feel angry or sad anymore.

He felt excited, because next year, he had another chance.

And this time, he would run not just to win, but to enjoy the race.

THE END.